SAFE
HAVEN

Why God Loves the Clinically Depressed

DEBBIE VANDERSLICE

WESTBOW
P R E S S®
A DIVISION OF THOMAS NELSON
& ZONDERVAN

This book is a work of non-fiction. Unless otherwise noted, the author and the publisher make no explicit guarantees as to the accuracy of the information contained in this book and in some cases, names of people and places have been altered to protect their privacy.

WestBow Press books may be ordered through booksellers or by contacting:

WestBow Press
A Division of Thomas Nelson & Zondervan
1663 Liberty Drive
Bloomington, IN 47403
www.westbowpress.com
844-714-3454

Because of the dynamic nature of the Internet, any web addresses or links contained in this book may have changed since publication and may no longer be valid. The views expressed in this work are solely those of the author and do not necessarily reflect the views of the publisher, and the publisher hereby disclaims any responsibility for them.

Any people depicted in stock imagery provided by Getty Images are models, and such images are being used for illustrative purposes only. Certain stock imagery © Getty Images.

Scripture quotations are from the ESV® Bible (The Holy Bible, English Standard Version®), Copyright © 2001 by Crossway, a publishing ministry of Good News Publishers. Used by permission. All rights reserved.

ISBN: 978-1-6642-4618-8 (sc)
ISBN: 978-1-6642-4617-1 (e)

Print information available on the last page.

WestBow Press rev. date: 11/10/2021

Hook: While the church many times shuns the depressed,
God emphatically opens His heart in Scripture time
and time again to these hurting individuals.

Dedication

To Hannah, Sherry, Leigh Anne, Quincy, Kay, Ann, and the entire gang at church...I shudder to think where I would be without you all. And to Cynthia, Chip, Mom. Edy, Gibbons, and boys...your generosity overwhelms me. I owe each of you a great debt, I will try to pay it forward.

About the Author

Debbie Vanderslice graduated from Southern Methodist University in Dallas, Texas, with a B.A. in history where she played tennis on a full scholarship. While there, she was a member of the history honor society and was a GTE Academic All American. With her strong writing skills and love for God, she has gone on to work freelance for such companies as DaySpring, Celebration, and Standard. Debbie has had Shameless, an indepth women's bible study, published by New Hope Publishers.

Debbie seeks to minister to hurting women who have gone through many trials and tribulations. Debbie, a survivor of abuse, has fought many personal battles, including an eating disorder, and is an active member of AA. Debbie's passion can be seen in the example of Jesus commanding others to take off Lazarus' grave clothes, as she seeks to help those trying to become free from past issues as well as personal mistakes. Her current book, Shameless, helps women overcome the obstacle of shame. Debbie is deeply committed to being a reality based writer who discusses real life issues women face today.

Debbie currently teaches and writes full time. Debbie is actively training for her second marathon. Debbie was a nationally ranked tennis player who won several state championships, was the eighth ranked amateur in the nation in 1989 in singles and was the third ranked doubles amateur in the nation in 1989. She has coached numerous state champions and has coached on the high school and college level. Debbie enjoys spending time with her family.

Overview

Safe Haven (Why God Loves the Clinically Depressed) is an eight chapter nonfiction book that examines why the church is so apt to shun the depressed, while God on the other hand, warmly invites them into His cause. It is no secret that there is a social stigma attached to those who are in treatment for depression. While some may argue that the church supports mental illness, the battling depression.

Safe Haven will statistically show that depression affects a multitude of people. Both men and women, not to mention adolescents, suffer physiological and emotional symptoms, while having to deal with the social petechia of depression. Safe Haven will give scriptural proof of how God compassionately touched the lives of the depressed while including them into His ministry.

Safe Haven is written for the millions and millions of men and women who have been cast off by the Church for their diagnoses of depression. This book will explore the medical causes of depression as well as its symptoms and treatment courses. This book will serve as a haven for those who have grown weary of hiding who they are and what they have. This book opens its arms and gives credence to all those who bravely live with depression while living in a religious society that closes its eyes.

Chapter 1 An Insidious Foe: This opening chapter explores the medical and emotional causes and symptoms of depression. It is imperative that each reader understand the physiological causes of depression before delving into the social stigma attached to it. Readers will see how they, or someone they know, suffer from depression.

Chapter 2 The First Missionary: This chapter highlights the first New Testament missionary...the man to cut himself in the tombs and broke his chains. This chapter gives proof of how Jesus took the time to care for this mentally unstable man, healed him, and then sent him off to give his testimony to others. Readers will see firsthand how God did not choose a pastor, stay at home mother, lawyer, doctor, or student to go tell others about Him. He scripturally used this depressed man to be the first New Testament missionary.

Chapter 3 The Woman Who Bled for 12 Years: The next point in case comes from the woman who endured twelve long years of hemorrhaging. By looking at the physical symptoms this woman went through, as well as the emotional toll on her body, readers will see that this woman definitely qualified as depressed. One must also factor in the reality that scripture says she had spent all she had on doctors. Thus, when you combine the physical, emotional, and financial havoc that was placed on this woman, it was a wonder she was still alive.

Chapter 4 Getting Real, Getting Honest: This chapter parleys what the church must do in order to support those suffering from depression. By honestly looking at depression from not merely a spiritual component, but instead by examining the medical causes it is, then, the church can truly begin to foster a spirit of true humanity.

Chapter 5 Accepting the Truth: This chapter zeroes in on Christ's words in John 8:32 "you shall know the truth, and the truth shall set you free." It is only when the church firmly accepts depression into its midst, that true healing for its believers can take place.

Chapter 6 The Real Deal: This chapter zeroes in how the church can show true concern and care about its members who are suffering from depression. Instead of telling those who suffer from depression to "count their blessings," or to "put on a happy face," reality based concern is instead encouraged.

Chapter 7 Go Tell it on the Mountain: This chapter focuses on educating the masses. The church should be the primary facilitator in educating others about depression. While this may sound unusual, why then did Christ continue to heal those suffering from depression as it relates to the religious masses around him? It is only by incorporating this often looked condition into the church, that true healing can take place. Why shouldn't the church be the primary source of education for a disease that plagues at one time, 20% of the population for women?

Chapter 8 Walking the Path of Peace: In this concluding chapter, an admonition to all those who suffer from depression is given: whether the church rises to the forefront or not, they are encouraged to simply be who they are and what they have. Just as it took education and tolerance for segregation to fall, and just as it took years and years for others to accept AIDS, so too those of us who suffer from depression must hold steadfast in the hope that one day their congregations will accept and love those who Christ commissioned long ago.

Marketing Section-Who Will Buy This Book and Why

The following statistics account for depression:

- The prevalence rate for depression in the U.S. is approximately 1 in 18 or 5.30% of the population, or 14.4 million people. (National Institute of Health, NIH, 1998)

- 6.7 million women have a major depression disorder in the U.S. (NIH, 1998)
- 3.2 million men have a major depression disorder in the U.S. (NIH, 1998)

- 10% in the U.S. alone of the country's population of age 18 and older develop depressive symptoms. (NIH, 1998)

- Lifetime risk of a depression episode is 20% for women (USSG, 1998)
- Annually 12% of women have a depressive episode (USSG, 1998)
- Annually 7% of men have a depressive episode (USSG, 1998)

- 4% of adolescents get seriously depressed each year (USSG, 1998)

When AIDS was first diagnosed and made public in the 1970's and 1980's there was widespread panic. Patients were often discriminated against, avoided, and harassed by an ignorant public. Depression, much like AIDS, has made impressive progress in its diagnoses, treatment, and causes. If we, as a church, are to stand together with those impacted from depression, then education, inclusion, and acceptance must be welcomed by the church. This book will be bought by the millions and millions of people affected directly and indirectly by depression. These readers long for a book that admonishes the church, while at the same time proving scripturally that Jesus did indeed welcome the clinically depressed. Readers who long to be validated will buy this book.

Competition Section

There has been relatively little written about depression and the church in terms of books. However, much has been written in terms of articles about depression and the church. There is one resource on the market today, written in 2004, that addresses some of my book's concerns. Surviving Depression: A Catholic Approach was written by Kathryn James Hermes and published by Pauline Books and Media.

Their book concerns itself with how to deal with depression. It uses the Catholic Church as a remedy in aiding those who suffer from depression.

However, my book addresses the concern about the lack of support from the church and then uses the Bible to validate how Christ indeed walked and talked with those who were depressed. There is no current book on the market that uses or points to scriptural references to urge its plea for help from the Church. My book makes the assertion that if Christ found time to support those who were clinically depressed, then surely the church has the fortitude to take up this cause.

Chapter 1

An Insidious Foe

Maybe you saw it today. That thin lady who runs morning, noon, and night. Or maybe it's the coworker who tells the tale that he hasn't slept in over a week. Or just maybe it gets a little more personal. Maybe you know depression all too well. Maybe you saw it in the mirror this morning. Perhaps you know the signs and symptoms of depression. Maybe it runs in your family. Or maybe after a life altering event, you now sleep with the enemy of depression. Take heart friend. This is a refuge. A safe haven. Maybe even the unthinkable has happened. Perhaps you have been cast off into the sea of forgetfulness by someone you thought would stand by your side. The church. Maybe, just maybe, this book can give you hope again. Hope that says Christ wants you, even if the church closes its door on your knocking. So, sit back, breathe deep, and watch as we summon The One who hung out with the depressed.

It is important to first tell what depression is clinically, its symptoms, causes, and treatment source. Without this key component, others who shun the depressed will never become educated as to what they are dismissing merely as a spiritual condition. Depression goes much deeper than that. It is a medical condition above all else.

The primary features of depression are a predominately sad mood and loss in day to day activities. Other symptoms include difficulty concentrating, hopelessness, guilt, worthlessness, and even anger or irritability. Depressed people often experience chronic fatigue or pain. Chronic pain is closely associated with depression because both the mood and pain perception centers are located in the same area of the brain. Chronic pain and depression can rob the body's stores of endorphins and other neurochemicals. Over 75% of patients with depression have complaints of physical pain as well. Depression is caused by a combination of things. It is the result of an imbalance of chemicals called neurotransmitters that carry signals to the brain and nerves. When the brain and body are deprived of these neurotransmitters, depression occurs. Combined with a variance of life given situations, symptoms will occur.

Unless the church admits that depression is a real, viable medical condition that originates in the brain and then is released into the body, no advances toward compassion and healing can take place in the walls of spiritual help. I cannot tell you how many times I have heard the phrase, "well, just pick yourself up and get going," or "it's not that bad," or "stop feeling sorry for yourself." If a clinically depressed person could change his feelings he would.

Psychotherapy and medication must go hand in hand. Such medications as help by correcting the imbalance in the brain that includes serotonin, norepinephrine, and dopamine. All these neurotransmitters function within areas of the brain that regulate emotions and mood. A skilled psychotherapist can help a depressed patient explore what all is going on in his life that may contribute to his depression. When combined with medication the outlook is very favorable.

The church's lack of response to psychiatric illnesses is an understatement. Until the church opens its eyes and acknowledges that depression is first a medical condition, just like diabetes, there will be no change. Those who suffer from depression will go from church to church seeking validity, or worse, will sit in the pews in secrecy, hiding who they really are and what they really suffer from.

- ■ In the U.S. alone, over 18.8 million American adults, or 9.5% of population, have a depressive disorder.

- Nearly twice as many women, 12.0%, as men 6.6%, are affected by a depressive disorder

- Depression affects all people of age, geographic location, demographic or social position

- A recent study sponsored by the World Health Organization found depression to be the leading cause of disability in the U.S.

- Women between the ages of 25-44 are most often affected by depression with a major cause of depression in women being the inability to express or handle anger.

- Depressive disorders are appearing earlier in life with the average age of onset 50 years ago being 29, whereas recent statistics indicate it at just 14.5 years in today's society.

- Up to 2.5% of children in the U.S. suffer from depression

- In 1997, suicide was the leading cause of death of 10-24 year-olds. All too often suicide is the result of extended periods of depression.

- While major depressive disorder can develop at any age, the average age of onset is the mid-20's.

You probably picked up this book for a specific reason. One, you want to stop hiding from depression and ironically, the church only adds fuel to this fire. Two, you want to find solace in the fact that Christ hung out with the clinically depressed. Or three, someone you love suffers from depression and you want to help. All three are valid reasons for picking up this book. I wrote it for very personal reasons. I have struggled with depression for over twenty years. I was fired from my last job for being hospitalized with depression. This book is my weak attempt to communicate to the world that while the church hides its head in the sand as far as how to treat those with depression, Christ was very clear on his intent with the mentally ill. He will unashamedly use them, their illnesses, and its message to show the true compassion the church should be exhibiting. That is why I wrote this book. Come with me as we go a little deeper and more personal with depression.

Chapter 2

The First Missionary

Who was the first missionary commissioned by Christ. A doctor? Lawyer? Stay at home mother? Priest? No. You are way off. Are you ready for it? It was a deranged man who cut on himself and lived among the tombs. The Gospel is not for the timid at heart. It is messy. Or rather, He takes our tattered lives and weaves a beautiful tapestry just for us. Let us take a look at the first New Testament missionary Jesus called.

He lived among the dead with their graves who gave no gossip. Just dead people in their resting place. The dead people do not gossip about him or cause him any trouble. He rather liked living in the tombs. Yes, he cut on himself to feel something. Anything. Even pain was welcomed by this emotionally unstable man. He just wanted to be alive, but the tombs say otherwise. He lived among the dead. He felt the same thing they did. Nothing.

I knew a cutter in junior high and high school. He was popular and handsome. He made ok grades. And he cut on his arms and wrists. And frequented the local mental hospital. Guess what he is doing today? He is a missionary counselor to his hometown; to the kids at his same high school He doesn't merely sympathize with them, he emphasizes with them. He doesn't merely shout I know, he whispers I understand to the cutters of this generation. You go man. You go.

The man in the tombs was emotionally unstable. He belonged in a mental hospital if they would have had such a thing back then. He could have stayed home but he got kicked out his last episode. He found the one place that brought him some solace. The cemetery was the place where he could find some peace. And he could rant and rave all he wanted to. Yes, he heard voices and was delusional but did it hurt any one? No. Just him.

Enter Jesus. Jehovah Rapha, the Lord who heals. The man in the tombs, life was about to change once he encountered Christ. "They came to the other side of the sea, to the country of Gerasenes. And when Jesus had stepped out of the boat, immediately there met him out of the tombs a man with an unclean spirit. He lived among the tombs. And no one could bind him anymore, not even with a chain, for he had often been bound with shackles and chains, but he wrenched the chains apart, and he broke the shackles in pieces. No one had the strength to subdue him. Night and day among the tombs and on the mountains, he was always crying out and cutting himself with stones. And when he saw Jesus from afar he fell down before him and knew who He was...and Jesus did not permit him to go with Him, but to go home to your friends and tell them how much the Lord has done for you....and he began to proclaim in Decopolis how much Jesus had done for him. And everyone marveled." (Matthew 5:2-9 ESV)

This man had a reputation. No one came his way. He was crazy, nuts, mentally impaired. And so God chose him to be the very first missionary in his hometown in the New Testament. Hasn't he been through enough? Will they even listen to him? He showered and shaved and put on clean clothes. He wanted to go with Jesus out of town to the masses, but He said no go to your hometown. So he did just that. Scripture says, "...and everyone marveled." (Mark 5:9a)

Some of us go home. Who is there? Family and friends. A history with them. Some good memories and some bad memories. Maybe if we move away from the shame it will go away. It doesn't. I tried it for a couple of years. Even worked at a church. Shame is such a funny thing. It is locked from the inside out. We imprison ourselves. Going home is hard if there is the cycle of abuse. But oh, so potentially healing...that is if we let The Healer in on it. I say to you...you haven't seen anything yet...after an encounter with Jehovah Rapha..."The Lord Who Heals."

What can we learn from the first missionary of the New Testament? First we can bloom where we are planted. We can tell others our story and then the goodness of God's healing grace. Give credit where it is needed. No God doesn't need us we need Him. It was Jesus who healed this man of the tombs. He was so far gone that it must be something or someone who healed him. It was Christ and Christ alone who healed him.

Sometimes we forget to thank the Lord. We think it is all us, when it is not us at all. It is all about Him. Secondly, God will use what we have, not what we do not have. All the man in the tombs had was his mind. Not even clothes, but once he followed Jesus the clothes and a shaven man was presented to the people who he knew. Notice though, Jesus took this deranged man and touched him and viola he was fully dressed and clean. Why is that there? Jesus healed his smelly clothes and all. We don't have to get dressed up in order to encounter the Healer. I think just because we are instantly a believer that we have it all together or something to that effect. We envision Africa or Central America. But God calls us to have the biggest impact at home. That may be Africa or Central America. For me it is Little Rock, Arkansas right now. Oh I get tired of the same old city, but for this season of life I am here. I am trying to bloom where I am planted.

God will use what we have to offer to serve Him. He uses all of us. Every little thing. We do not have much, you think. Hold on for a moment. If we have fallen, and we all have, just get up again. And again. And again. Remember He picks us up off the floor. We are being sanctified. I wrote something about being refined. Situations come our way and we did not ask for them. Is the Father on His throne? Everything seems out of control. What good can come from this? It is called the sanctification process. God is refining us. Just like the blacksmith forges up the fire to get rid of the impurities, so too how will we handle God's molding us?

The Refining

"So that genuineness of your faith-more precious Than gold that
perishes through it is tested by Fire-may be found to result in
praise and glory And honor at the revelation of Jesus Christ."
(1Peter 1:7 ESV)

Sometimes this grief washes over me
like the ocean waves crashing against the sand.
Unending. Ceaseless. Perpetual. To the
mere spectator turned vacationer
the water brings with it peace, solitude, peace.
But to the resident who beaches upon
Its shore day after day month after month, The waves
carry pain loneliness and grief How long O Lord,
Will the waters captivate my life? My every
move? Thought? Response?
My world stopped while the world went rudely on.
My tears flowed unceasingly while others
seemed to smile effortlessly.
Where is my hope, O God? Why do these lips
honestly confess the horrors of my heart?

For whatever is gone now I can rest assured
that You are still in control,
and will one day reveal the seemingly painful
madness of the here and now,
to the overwhelmingly speechless perfection of your divine plan.
Your method is perfect. Your timing is perfect.
May this life of mine not tarry in vain
as I seek your hand during this molding process.
*(Debbie Vanderslice, Tate
Publishing, Dressing Up Death, p. 68-69, 2016 ESV)*

What will we go through during the refining phase of our life? Will it be cancer? The loss of a child? An illness that won't go away until that glorious day when we see Christ face to face? Whatever the hardship is, we can be sure of this...God loves us too much to not use bad for good. He will use every single bit of suffering we have and make something beautiful of it. Take it to the bank. God will use whatever we have, no matter the flaws and turn it into His Glory. It is all about Him, not us.

It is through hardships that we grow close or closer to God. Take again my missionary minded friend, Martha. She down played her cancer, a small melon, embedded in her chest while pregnant. The doctors said abort and she said no.So she endured 5 straight months of chemo and radiation and a med a port in her chest, all without a numbing shot. For Madison's sake, her unborn baby girl, she took as little as possible.

As we were playing cards lucky 7 and 21, in the hospital,I learned that I have no patience at all. Martha was in pain and seizing again. I looked out her door and found a nurse. The urgency in my voice gave the nurse reason to run towards Matha's door. She came back with a bevy of doctors and nurses. I was asked to wait outside the door. I complied. Martha's mom arrived 10 minutes later. I told her that Martha had another seizure. As we both held hands, Martha's mom told me what a good friend I had been to her daughter. I asked her how did she know. She said no other friend had bought a 25 dollar gift certificate to the sno cone stand. People just don't do that." But I said, "Martha needed something to soothe her sore throat from radiation. I thought flavored ice would be good for her sore throat."

God can use us to be "domestic" missionaries. Bloom in the here and now. Not some pie in the sky. Yes, God may be calling you to go outside the country, but that is not for everyone. If you ask God where He wants you then watch out. God answers prayers in three ways. Yes, no, and wait. It is really that simple. God is not a God who uses formulas. You cannot figure it all out. No one can. But He is faithful and His burden is not too heavy for us. The Gospel is easy. Living it out is hard. He doesn't want cookie cutter believers, but real, live, individuals who love Him and call us each for a ministry.

Notice the man in the tombs wanted to go and travel with Christ once Jesus healed him. But Christ had other plans. He wanted the man in the tombs to go back to his hometown. Not Asia or Africa. But his hometown. There everyone knew him and his illness. He was a "domestic missionary." Ask God where you are to serve Him during your life today? It may be a wild ride, but God is faithful… He will equip us as He sends us wherever we are to be right now and even in the future.

After Martha died I continued to take care of Martha's son in a trade out. Martha's mom kept Madison. The rest of us kept her son, Dane, who was my daughter's age. Just 6 months between them. Carrie kept Dane too. We were all trying to hang onto Martha, be it her kids, car, or house. Maybe if we wished her hard enough she would come back. Was it a dream? A bad one at that. Martha's mom paid me the highest compliment ever. She said out of all the friends who loved Martha, I loved her the most.Why was that? I explained to her that I did not have time to invest in friendship when I was growing up, just tennis. I wanted to do this friendship right. Martha was my first best friend. The very first. I wrote this after Martha died.

The Friendship Tears

Isaiah 25:8 ESV

I come to you with
Unashamed friendship tears to weep.
You never tell me to stem them, Only to pour them at your feet.

She was a light down here
For just a short while
I never dreamed the race she would run
On behalf of heaven's mile.

Tenderness, touch and trust Were ours indeed
to share You frees my soul to love
As it was brokenly laid bare.

Many years I asked you
What friendship was all about
You opened Heaven's graceful gate and whispered
Martha's name with evidence of a shout.

So deaf did I become
As I begged for time to keep,
"This my precious child is proof of my love For you
because I have given you friendship tears to weep."
(Debbie Vanderslice, Shameless, New Hope Publishers, 1998 p. 49)

When we say the church or someone was full of glory, we are saying they are full of Christ and all of His goodness. We are especially of this in His Tabernacle in the Old Testament. We know now, today,that the church is not just four walls. It is the body of Christ wherever believers are, or meet. Glory is the presence of God. That can be anywhere. In the location of a prison, in a coffee shop in Brooklyn, or a homeless shelter in Los Angeles.

Jesus will go to Hades and back to save one sinner. Truly there is not anywhere He won't go to save one sinner. Glory or God's presence, can be anywhere, at any time, and in any form or fashion. I get so mad when I hear a believer say we must be qualified in order to serve God. Nothing is further from the truth. God used a Jesus hater named Paul to pen more than ¾ of the New Testament. Then there was an adultery by way of King David and Bathsheba. Not to mention Mary His mother.Then there is you and me. Yes, if you have trusted in Christ, God uses you too.God uses the most unlikely candidates to carry out His divine plan. It is all about Christ, and zero about us..." (The Treasures of Darkness, 2019, Westbow, Debbie Vanderslice, p.43, ESV)

So take heart my friend, you are in awesome company. Have you been a Christ hater. So was Paul. and David, and Bathsheba and the list goes on and on. Next time you feel unworthy go to God. If you have gone outside the bond of marriage, go to Him. Don't know how you are going to pay the bills, go to God. Difficult pregnancy? Go to God. Not enough food to make it to the next week? Go to God. Sometimes I think He is the last resort. Go to Him, but many times, relief comes in the saving grace of His people or the church. Instead of expecting manna to fall from the sky, why not seek out a food ministry?

We are "domestic" missionaries. Some of us are called to minister to other countries. Either way we all share in the Good News of Christ. Notice God healed the man in the tombs. He wanted to go with Jesus and travel for Him. But God had other plans. Go to his hometown and witness there. He bloomed where he was planted. That may be Africa or your hometown. When God sends us out He also equips us to be used by Him. Just ask the psychotic man in the tombs. He was being used by God. We can expect no less today.

Chapter 3

The Woman Who Bled for 12 years

Imagine girls/women that you are having your period not one year straight but twelve long years. It is hard for me to wrap my head around it. And they didn't have tampons during this Biblical time frame.It is in the Bible for us. Just for us and those who love us. She, the woman who bled for twelve years, faced many dilemmas.

First she was unceremonial unclean to go to worship at the temple. All she could do was help her father gather enough lambs for sacrifice to the priests and others who wanted to sacrifice an animal in worship. Usually, a lamb. It would not break the bank but it, the money, would keep them afloat another month or two. She was 12 years old when she last went to worship at the temple. Momma cried herself sick. Started her period that very year. Now it was non stop. As in all the time. All Momma knew to do was to wash the rags out. There were strips and strips of bloody cloths. That, and gather their best lambs for purchase by mainly the priests for worship. She could not go with her father into the temple. Only priests, merchants, and money lenders. No women allowed. So she waited a good distance from the temple. How was Father doing? Always thinking of others, she longed for the day she could wait beside her father and offer morale support to her father...and not be on the outside looking in.

She had heard that The Healer, Jesus, was coming to their city soon. Maybe today. Maybe she could just touch Him or His robe and be healed of this awful ailment. Just maybe today. Not a month from today or year or even decade. But today.

"And behold, a woman who had suffered from a discharge of blood for twelve years came up behind him and touched the fringe of His garment, I will be made well. Jesus turned and seeing her he said, " take heart daughter, your faith has made you well. And instantly the woman was made well" (Matt. 9:20-22, ESV) We can learn many things in His infallible Word in this passage.

First of all this woman was to bloom where she was planted. She did just that. Did she not gather the best lambs for market from her father's pasture? She could have just gathered any old lamb. But Father wanted the best for market. Funny though, the priests, not all, but many, would choose a blemished lamb and then Father would go down on the price.

Secondarily, Daddy was very progressive as far as women. He treated her with respect. He let her and his sons choose the lambs for sale to be sacrificed as an offering to the Lord. Even though many people thought of her as an outcast, he treated her the same as if she were as good as some of the other merchants' sons. She was as smart as a whip. Until the other merchants threatened to not let her accompany her father to the temple/market. His livelihood for the entire family rested on his job. He made the gut wrenching decision of leaving her at home. It was definitely a no win decision.

Enter The King of Kings. He knows all and sees all. He got so mad at the merchants making a buck off His Father, as well as women. He turned over the tables and threw out the money lenders. No one would make a buck today, if He sought fit. His whip saw to that. Jesus left and she followed, bloody clothes and all. She thought, "if i can just touch the fringe of His robe." Instantly she was healed. After a full decade of bleeding she just stopped. All it took was one word from Jesus. So now her family would be ok to worship as a family now. It is strange, but Christ knew immediately why she was trying to touch his robe. He sees all. He knows all. He is the long awaited Messiah.

Here was a bloody woman who knew Jesus could heal her. Heck, it couldn't hurt her could it? She had been to all kinds of healers and it worked...for about 24 hours then back to bleeding again. On the rag once again. But there was something different about this healer. His eyes met hers and she knew then that He was The One. Jehovah Rapha, the Lord that Heals.

He knew she had spent all her money and the family's funds on all kinds of faith healers. Emotionally she had no friends to confide in. Spiritually, she had left God a long time ago. Or should we say years ago. There were no gentlemen callers at her door. She was stuck in her situation. Until that day when her eyes met His eyes. There was something different about this faith healer. People were all a buzz about Him. Did He really do miracles? She sure could use one right about now. Blood means life. She sure did have enough of it. Was their life amidst all her blood? And He healed outside the temple. Was He really the long awaited Messiah? He looked pretty normal to her. Why was everyone talking about Him? Some say a prophet. Or maybe a medicine man, or is He the long awaited Messiah?

Whomever He was she wanted in. He made her stop bleeding. Instantly. Today. Immediately. Now. She was healed after 12 years of nonstop bleeding. Now she was ceremonially clean. The spotless lamb had healed her. She got her life back. All it took was Christ. How could she pay Him back for giving her life back to her? Now she could go with Father to the temple and participate in selling lambs to the masses. Now she could hang out with friends and family. Now she wasn't an untouchable, like the lepers. She could live again. All it took was Jesus healing her. She could even follow Him, but could do more good here in her hometown. He was her safe haven. He was it. No longer looking for a cure. He was the answer to everything. He was the long awaited Messiah.

Read and write out the following verses

Exodus 12:13

Lev. 17:14

Romans 5:9

What do all these verses have in common? They are powerful. Timely. Relevant. What today can we learn from these versus?

Blood. Pure and simple. An animal had to be sacrificed to atone for the sins of the people. Jesus was our Passover Lamb. What? Every year during Passover the angel of death would pass over the households of those who had blood on their door frames. Thus it was called The Passover. Jesus was called the ultimate passover lamb. His shed blood was enough for the angel of death to passover those who trusted in Him. Pretty cool, huh? He truly is our safe haven. Our safety in storms, good weather, ice, rain, scorching heat, you name it God did it for yesteryear why not do it today? He does and He is our Passover Lamb.

Chapter 4

Getting Real and Getting Honest

It happens in every church. Every school. Every workplace. Every home. It is practically everywhere. It affects over 6 million people every year. Plus the toll on the family. That is at least 12 million more. What is it? Cancer? Car accidents? Heart disease? It is simply depression. It touches every domain. Every class. Every financial class. It is your dirty little secret called depression.

"Oh that would never happen to me, I am too well grounded."

"I am too tough and rough to ever have that," expounds the pastor of a large church. Yep, even he gets depression later on in his life

Clinical depression affects all races, creeds and economical status. If Christ is on the throne then how do we get this disease? I am glad you asked. I have a logical answer to that very question. As in chapter one I describe in depth what exactly is depression. It is above all else a physical condition. A skilled doctor can do blood work to determine if you have depression or not, along with a skilled therapist. Together they can determine if you are depressed or just stuck in a rut. I heard it from the pulpit...that depression is a spiritual condition. That same pastor was recently diagnosed with depression. He did a lot of back tracking. It is a physical condition. If you broke your leg you would go to the doctor. Same applies if you are down every day and over/under eat, no sleep, or sad most of the time. You would not play around with a broken femur, so why should you suffer in silence when your emotions are all messed up?

I have spent over 3 decades being depressed. I have tried it all. Even shock therapy. Several times. I have been on medication for my depression. Perhaps it was at bay all the years I played division I tennis. I simply did not have time to be depressed or even think during my high school and college years. Oh, there was time, but I just stuffed down my emotions. I got married when I was a merely 19 years old and played on a full tennis scholarship all four years. Life was grand, until I stopped playing tennis. It, tennis, was the main distraction. Not to mention taking 15 hours a semester in addition to travelling with tennis. When I stopped playing tennis my depression was not at bay. It was staring me in the face head on.

Yet another benefit of being in a safe haven is the understanding of Jesus' ways. Let me see if I can paint a picture for you. You are in a terrible car accident. Both legs, the femurs, are severely broken. You need immediate surgery or you will lose both legs. Or at the best walk with a limp the rest of your life. Without surgery you will die. Some choice, huh? You opt for surgery. The doctors were right, a severe limp it is. Choices are the cornerstone of life. Without choices we would not be here. Once you taste of freedom, it is addictive. You must have it. You crave it. You would even kill for it.

Jesus is 100% for following His ways. If we don't get psychological help when we need it, all heck breaks loose. It just festers and festers like a bad sore on our body. Unless that wound is properly cleaned out it becomes infected and pus grows underneath that sore. It can be large or small. It is the same. Infected. It just grows and grows. Let's get back to the leg story.

You opt for surgery on the legs. It will be much more painful than if you did not have surgery. But, you wouldn't walk very well. If you did do surgery you would have a chance of only walking with a slight limp. It is a hard choice but a slight limp is better than death. Anything is better than infection and death. You choose surgery. Life.

The verse John 8:32 says "if we shall know the truth, then the truth shall set us free." (John 8:32, ESV). The key word here is know, it doesn't mean know hi hum, it means to consummate the truth.

That requires action as in knowing, or knowing intimate. Once we do, do, do, something with the truth then we can be set free. It is not until an action is done that we can truly be set free. Can you relate friend? Freedom=truth+action.

Have you ever gone to eat with an old friend from grammar school or high school? They talk nonstop and are the expert on whatever you share. It gets old very quickly. Same year different verse. You and her have not changed a bit in over 30 years. You said all you had to say...1 hour ago. Your friend has gone on for over 2 hours. And she comments, "you shouldn't feel that way," or she can relate and she shares 1 and1/2 hours on your topic. I cannot stand this type of friend. She knows it all and knows what is best for you. All you wanted was cheese with your fajita. Nothing of substance is shared with her at all.

God wants us to be real with Him. In therapy it is the same way. I have been in therapy with an amazing woman. Never have I had the patience she has. I can't say anything to make her leave. She is in it for the long haul and so am I. Same goes for the psychiatrist I see. I am on a winning team with them on board.

Are you disappointed I see these two professionals? I am human. I mess up each and every day. Yet, God is still there. Much like these two professionals are. God forgives me. Just like they do. He is patient with me. Just like they are patient with me. If ever I need a Christ like response, they are there to give it. They listen. Just like Christ does. They walk the walk and I am so glad of this. They show me the love of Christ. That is priceless to me. I could never thank them enough. I will try my best to pay it forward. That is all I can do. That is the highest compliment I can give them. I remember what we have talked about and then live it out. Imitation is the highest compliment. I owe them a debt I could never repay.

I say get in therapy and go see a psychiatrist. You will be like a new person. It has done wonders for me. I get real and honest with them. Won't you do the same today? If you have already done this I say "way to go. Now barf all over them." That is my refuge. They are my refuge. And it is ok with God. Some pastors say Christ is enough for him and he doesn't need therapy or doctors. I say to him, "Christ wants us to get over things done to us and change. I admonish you to go to the professionals. You will be glad you did. It saved my life. Many times they saved my life. God used them and still are. I wouldn't trade their advice for anything in the world.

Look up these verses and memorize them. If you feel guilty seeing a therapist, then put these verses on your fridge, or some place you frequent often. Hmmm. Yes, ma'am the fridge is where I keep mine. Hmmm.

Psalm 33:11 " The counsel of the Lord stands forever, the plans of His heart to all generations." (ESV)

Jeremiah 32:19a (ESV) "...great in counsel and mighty in deed..."

Isaiah 9:6b (ESV) "...and the government shall be upon His shoulder, and his name shall be called Wonderful Counselor, Mighty God, Everlasting Father, Prince of Peace."

Proverbs 24:66 (ESV) "...for by wise guidance you can wage your war, and in abundance of counselors there is victory."

It is wise to seek counsel when making big decisions. I go to my trusty therapist and doctor. Not to mention a few best buddies. I don't just make a rash decision. I call on my team for guidance. Being rash only leads to mistakes and I don't want to make bad decisions like where to live, what job to take, and so on. Those are big decisions to me. I make plenty of mistakes by being rash.but hindsight is 20/20.

We have to be careful when seeking professional help. Just because they have initials behind their name doesn't mean they are qualified. I knew a lady who had not passed the LPC three times. Licensed Professional Counselor. She could not pass it. So what did she do? She went to work for a church and was under someone who had passed the LPC test and was established. She said she was not seeking the LPC because she did not agree with the secular part. Truth be told, she could not pass it. I would not go near her for counseling. One way to get around it is the be under someone who has and hang your shingle out as a professional when in fact they have not passed the LPC test. It is totally legal to do this, but

I say keep looking for a kind, sensitive and caring Ph.D. It is merky water to say the least seeing someone with a master's degree only. I know I will get a lot of flack over this but my worst experience with counseling have been with a therapist with a master's degree. He/ She does most of the talking and say over and over, "you shouldn't feel that way" or the likes there of. They have all the answers. Or at least that has been my experience with these kinds of therapists. They are as clueless and phony as their qualifications. They give fake advice. Only lining their wallets with your payments. Some, not all, are like this. I thank God for the two professionals in my life. They are real and their faith is real. No need to flaunt their credentials. Time and time again they have shown me what Christ is really like. They have provided me a refuge from my wearily legs. When I see them I see Christ.

Was Christ ever depressed? I think so. All His friends or disciples deserted Him. Where were His friends, Mary of Bethany, Martha the busy domestic goddess, and raised from the dead Lazarus? Where they nearby when they were nailing Him to a tree. The answer may surprise you. The answer is no they were not there. Maybe it was just too much for His good buddies. I have a theory. God does not give us more than we can bear. This includes these three individuals who loved Christ the most. Out of the billion people He could have reappeared to He chose Mary, Martha, and Lazarus. Not family. Not the 12 disciples. Just three ordinary people. I like that. How about you?

Chapter 5

Accepting the Truth

This chapter zeroes on the verse John 8:32 "You shall know the truth and the truth shall set you free." (ESV) It is only when the church finally accepts depression is a medical condition, that true healing for its' believers can then experience true healing.heart.

If the truth sets us free why then are we not free, after all we keep quoting this verse over and over. We have to dig a little bit. As in the Greek language. The Old Testament was written in the Hebrew language and The New Testament in the Greek language. It is all about translation. I recommend a Strong's concordance for translation. That and a King James bible or translation. It will do wonders for your daily reading. It will transform your quiet times.

If we know the truth then why are we not free.The key word here is KNOW. It uses this word specifically here. It means to know as in consummation. To know every bit of the body. As in sexual relations between husband and wife. What? You are saying the greek word here means the consummation of husband and wife? That is exactly what God is saying here. So we are to know, know, know the truth inside and out, just like sexual relations between the two. Wow, I did not know that Deb. I know, me too. God is into details and we should expect no less in this Scripture.

So to know the truth requires action, just like sexual relations. I can know I am a drug abuser but until I do something with the truth like go to a meeting I am not knowing the truth. In Scripture, this word to know means action. Do you have something you need to know, requiring action. It is then we are set free. Not merely acknowledging the truth. But doing something with the truth.

There are no gray areas in God's Word. It is pretty cut and dry. If you don't believe me then try it yourselves. Choose a topic and then go to town with a concordance and a KJV of the Bible and see for yourself. It may surprise you. There is nothing new under the sun, or so it goes.I like the book makers that say what you are feeling and then put an appropriate verse to it. It is very helpful. Try memorizing the verses on the topic you like at the line at the grocery store or waiting in line in the bank, and so on. Do this and you have quit the doubting game into the winner's game.

"Eve did not merely tremble when she heard God walking in the Garden That fateful day. She was physically, emotionally, and spiritually terrified to the point of never wanting to see her Creator face to face again. So when He asked her what she had done, Eve lowered her shame-ridden, darting eyes and gave what she had never given before. An excuse as well as a lie.The serpent deceived me and I ate."

It wasn't a total lie. Satan had deceived her Eve immediately despised not only herself, but also what she had done, and especially what she was doing now; covering by the bushes in the bushes in the darkness of sin instead instead of walking in the light with her Creator hand and hand through the Garden

Eve thoughtlessly in a second traded who God had intended her to be and bought the lie of all time...that she was defected to the very core of her being. The game of sin, darkness, were the players who presented themselves. It would take God's own Son being crucified publically to bring back truth and light to all who would venture down Satan's unending road..." (Shameless, New Hope Publishing, 2016, p.34-35 ESV)

You hate to be around her. But you share a cubicle with her at work. Everything is not her fault. Or so she says. You hate sharing lunch, usually an hour or so., with her next door. So you moved this party outside. She would not venture outside would she? Yes, she would. She follows you around like a pup dog in search of a dog biscuit. Yep, no privacy. When you have to use the facilities she is right there with you. She likes you and you are the only one who will listen to her.

I had used this example before but it bears repeating. There was a certain pastor in a large suburb of Dallas who was faithful each Sunday to give his weekly sermon. He never missed. His problem became their problem. He said jump and they said how high. He said from the pulpit that he never would have depression because he was "too well grounded." That comment set me back about ten years. What then are we who struggle with depression to do? The church often shames us to get over it or we care just feeling blue. Maybe true healing comes in the form of therapy or medication. Or, alas, both.This particular pastor changed his tune when he was diagnosed with clinical depression. Unfortunately this pastor is influential in many ways. Now about fifteen thousand church goers believe as he does...that depression is real. Not some doctors' pie in the sky believing. It is real. How sad that 25% of his congregation suffered in silence. It was not necessary for them to feel ashamed over their diagnosis of clinical depression, or the many other mental diagnoses out there. I wrote this when I was in was in deep depression. I could say in theory I have never been diagnosed with depression. I had to get help. I am a big believer in depression. It is hard to put on a happy face when your life is falling apart, which is what depression feels like. See if you can relate to this poem.

Somewhere

Somewhere along the path I lost my way Somewhere along
the way I lost my hope. Somehow without my hope, I found
resentment Somehow my resentment turned to anger.
Somehow my anger frew into bitterness. Somehow my
bitterness flew into rage. Somehow my rage consumed me.
Somehow in the rage consumed me. Somehow in
the rage, I blamed you, O God For all the pain.

For all the abandonment.
For all the fear. For all the sorrow.
For all the grief. For all the tears. For all the dreams never lived.

For all the hopes left unfulfilled.
Do you know O God,how difficult this is for me?
To take your hand and trust you in what I cannot see.
You know my past and pain so well, For it is real to me.
Can you take my tattered life
And help me live for all eternity?

Somewhere along the road O Lord, I gave my heart.
Somewhere along the trodden path, I lost those that I loved.
If I give you my honesty
And choose to do what is right, Will you in turn give
me the strength To last the good and holy fight. Because
I come to you as a little child So very, very lost.
Someway along the way, I blamed you
For all the pain and thus the cost.

Debbie Vanderslice Shameless, New Hope
Publishing p. 31-32 2008 Dressing
Up Death,Tate Publishing

Accepting the truth is hard. It is a bitter pill to swallow at age 30 running a marathon while pregnant and then facing lymphoma cancer the next day. It is a different kind of marathon to run in while undergoing chemo and radiation at age 30. It was for me. Not so with Martha. It is like being with an open Bible with her. She never once said, "why me, God?" I would go home and cry and cry after I was with her. The Scriptures poured out of me after being around her. Phrases like"drink offering, and I lay down my life" and so on came forth from me straight from the Bible. Each was indicative of God and His Word. Surely, Martha was His child and was just grand-standing to make it more of His glory. But I was wrong. Oh, Martha was His child and unfortunately called her home late in November. November 19. 1998. I will forever remember getting the call that she had passed away. As I hung up the phone I noticed it was beginning to snow. Earliest snow ever in Texas. As if God were telling me "'yes she is with me. She lived a pure life Deb, I have her now. She is no longer hooked up to machines or in pain. She is running with me, the King of Kings. Lord of Lords, I am Jehovah Rapha, the Lord who heals...she is with me Deb. She is ok. I have her here with me."

This is a bad yet useful example of knowing the truth that sets on free. You wake up one gloomy, hazy morning and do not feel like a female. You check all the body parts and lo and behold you are a female. Plain and simple. But you cried and cried to the Lord that you wanted to be a boy. If you want to become a man you would need to do something with the truth that kept you from being a boy. Many surgeries and counseling were in the works for you. First however, you must go through the many hoops that are necessary for your transformation to take place.

I don't think these individuals wake up and say today I am being made a female/male. If they know the truth and it says they will be free, freedom isn't achieved just paying lip service. There must be action included. For Karen, this meant surgery. Expensive? Yes. right or wrong, it is done.God requires action if truth is going to set us free. Until the congregation of mainstream religion accepts these individuals as they are or will be, we are not accepting them as Jesus would. My first book, Shameless, was about the 8 people/ women God listed in the genealogy of Jesus. Not your garden club ladies, either. Very messy women with a past. One requirement was that they were honest. Are we honest and truthful in all our day to day living. I think not. How about when driving. I can gauge my temperament on the driver who cut me off. Do I give prudence to him or let him slide. What would Jesus Do? So love is always the answer. Truth always prevails. Light over darkness. A scared woman dressing in drag in your church or having a sex change operation is accepted. I would like to think he/she is welcome in your church. Doesn't God use the devil worshippers, women of the veils, teeny boppers, wedding vow breakers, murders??? And the list can and does go on and on. God yes, the one on the throne uses you and me to carry out His divine purposes. He is making all things beautiful in His own time. See below

Eccl 3:11 " He has made all things beautiful in its' time (ESV)

Memorize it. Put it on the fridge. On the dashboard of your car.

In the bathroom. Wherever you frequent all the time. Memorize one a week. I promise it will revolutionize your life. God Word will soothe your soul like nothing else.

Memorize these verses or better yet four. My favorite ones are as follows:

Romans 8:28 " And we know that for those who love God all things work together for good, for those are called all things work together for good." (Romans 8:28b, ESV)

(ESV)

Philippians 4:13"I can do all things through Christ who strengthens me."

Genesis 50:20 'As for you, you meant evil against me, but God meant it for good" (ESV)

Job 13:15a "Though he slay me, I will hope in him."

Each verse is very different yet it fits perfectly here. Which one is your favorite? Why?

Chapter 6

The Real Deal

I knew a pastor of a pretty large church and it bears mentioning again, seriously, a mega church in the Dallas Ft. Worth, Texas, who went by the Word and lived it...he said over and over that depression was invented by man not of God at all. He said he was too well grounded to ever need medication...until he was diagnosed with the disease. Imagine those around him. He had lot of backtracking to do, and of course he did.

Now there are now Bible studies at this church that delves into depression in church-goers lives. All it took was this pastor getting it for the church to talk about it. And they did. Why were these people fooled? They are human as is their pastor. They had a lot to learn about depression. I, a mere female human, knew this and was light years ahead them. If they are fooled by Satan and depression what else has he said that is reversible for the congregation. Depression is far reaching and makes no distinction who you are. Even evangelical pastors get depression too.

I can think of no better example than Christ. He wore the robe of human being and think of all the things He had to endure or suffer through. He had to fight hunger. He was thirsty. He had to fight the urges of the opposite sex. Hold on. Hold on, Deb. God is sexual? Well, Scripture tells us He was tempted in *every* way and was without sin. Hmm. I know it sounds so human to have sexual temptations. But look at what Luke has to says, "And Jesus was led by the Spirit in the wilderness for forty days, being tempted by the devil." (Luke 4:1-3, ESV) So temptation is of Satan. God is not the author of temptation.

Perhaps the most bizarre thing in all the world I have experienced is the Incarnation. What exactly is it? It is where God becomes flesh. He left the all-you- can-eat buffet, not to mention the angels encircling the throne saying ' holy holy holy... It is where God the Son gives it all up to come down to earth as a mere mortal to engage them in different ways to spread His love for us. Anybody who takes my place of death, is AOK in my book. What was it like hanging there on the cross for you and me? What was it like to be The Truth and yet treated as a lie? What was it like to have been the Holy One and yet spit upon as unholy? What was it like to have been The Way and yet treated as the lost?

> "What was stolen secretly in the Garden so long ago would one day one be bought publicly by the blood of Jesus. Ever since the Garden of Eden, we have been broken. We were meant to live in the Garden with all the amenities had But curiosity killed the cat, and behold, Adam and Eve were kicked out of Eden. Into the world of sin. But notice what God does. He supplied them with a sacrifice, and God himself clothed them, what a benevolent god to provide clothes for them. A sacrifice of an animal was necessary for clothes to cover them." (The Dance of the Addiction p.86 Vanderslice) Tate Publishers

Sounds like another person who became our Lamb of God to cover our sins. Notice what Adam and Eve did during this event of God clothing them. Absolutely nothing. Just like them we do nothing. It is about Him and zero of us. All we do is believe in our heart. Let me tell you about my salvation day. No it was not where angels appeared. There was no light shining from above. It happened on the way to the bathroom. Come again you say. Yes, the bathroom. As I approached the throne I said, "come inside me Christ." I am sorry it wasn't more majestic. Did I say the sinner's prayer. No. Did I say it theoretically correct. No. But it was heartfelt. I received Him in all earnestness. I was 17 years old.

The impact was immediate. The most obvious was that I stopped cheating in school. My fellow classmates were shocked. While I did do worse in school, my confidence in my sport, tennis soared leaps and bounds. So did my rankings. I was 2nd in the Southern tournament in doubles and 2nd in singles. I played on the winning sectional team my junior year. I represented the South and we beat all the other sections. Life was grand. And then God threw a curve ball.

My tennis pro was hit by a car on his way to Florida for a tennis tournament when. Suffix to say his playing tennis was over. He was fighting for his life. Steel plates were put in his legs that were crushed on impact. The person whom I spent every afternoon with was now gone. He lived,but I was left without a pro. Enter in the SMU women's tennis coach. Although she was in Dallas, and I in Texarkana, Arkansas, we made monthly trips to Dallas to be taught tennis by her. She had several players come and I played sets with them. I won them all and was asked by her, to come aboard with them on a full tennis scholarship. It fit like a glove and I said yes. Out of something bad came something good.

Same can be true of Jesus' life. Out of the death of Jesus came life. He arose from the dead just like He said He would. People today do not have a noose around their neck. How silly you might say. It is a cross, once a dreaded symbol, now is worn by Christians to remind them of the love and sacrifice of what Christ did for them. Yes, what once was a symbol of defeat now is a symbol of love.Only God can take something bad, and make something beautiful out of it. Oh, my tennis grew leaps and bounds at this time in my life.

Life is all about the incarnation. God becoming flesh. Oh, we sing about it at Christmas time. O come O come Emmanuel, or God with us, God becoming Jesus, made flesh carried by a teenager who was pregnant, get this, with God. Did Mary know or not. All that was all conceived by the Holy Spirit? That one I will leave to the scholars. I like to think she, and eventually Joseph, knew. Maybe it was riding on the donkey trying to find a place to stop when she knew. Or maybe it was the wise men who brought the baby gifts from afar. Or maybe it was the star in the night for so long. Guiding them to Bethlehem. Or those, mainly Herod, who was trying to kill him and his family. Here are some of my favorite verses below.

1Peter 1:7 "So that the genuineness of your faith-more precious than gold that perishes though it is tested by fire-may be found to result in praise and glory and honor at the revelation of Jesus Christ."(ESV)

Read the following verses to yourself. Which one do you like the best out of them and ponder why.

> Ephesians 6: 12 "For we do not wrestle against flesh and blood, but against rulers, against the authorities, against the cosmic powers over this present darkness, against the spiritual of evil in the heavenly places." (ESV)

> Philippians 3:3 "For we are the circumcision who worship by the spirit of God and glory in Christ Jesus and put no confidence in the flesh..." (ESV)

> 1John 4:2 b ""By this you know the Spirit of God: and every spirit that confesses that Jesus Christ has come in the flesh is from God..." (ESV)

> John 1:14a "And the Word became flesh and dwelt among us..." (ESV)

Which verse is your favorite? Why?

Read the following passages from my book, Dressing Up Death. Hang in there. I do have a point to make.

"Our groaning is just a glimpse to the finality of the cross. Everything bad that happens to us can be used by God for His glory. And I do mean everything. What basis do I have for this bold claim? Only God's perfect Word.

Romans 8:28 (ESV) And we know that for those who love God, all things work together for good,for those who are called according to His purpose.".

A few years ago I cheated death. You can call it a near-death experience if you must. I call it a God thing. I had a massive stroke, and my heart stopped beating for two minutes. Before they shocked me back to life, here was my dream. I dreamed I was in a good place because I wasn't in any pain. I was in heaven. I had on a white robe that came down to my knees. Martha was there and had on the same thing. She had a bouquet of flowers I said, "Martha you've got hair!" "But of course," she replied.

I said, "Where are you going with those flowers?" She said, "To see the King, of course."

I said, "I want to go too."Martha laughed. "You can't, it is not your time yet."

And then she was gone. I will never forget that. I believe that was a near-death experience. I will never forget it. It remains the most vivid account of heaven and Martha was ok. I could rest now. Christ had her all along. Now I could move on. Somehow for some reason I needed to see both Martha and Christ. He knows me all too well.

"Ever since The Garden of Eden we have been broken.We were meant to live in the Garden with all the amenities it had. But curiosity killed the cat, and behold, Adam and Eve were kicked out of the Garden of Eden and thrown into the world of sin. But notice what God does. He supplied them with a sacrifice, and God Himself clothed them. What a benevolent God to provide clothes for them. He supplied them with a sacrifice, and God Himself clothed them. Notice what God does during the clothing of them.

Absolutely nothing. A sacrifice of an animal was necessary for clothes to cover Adam and Eve. Sounds like another story in the Bible who became our lamb of God to cover us in our sin. Just like Adam and Eve did nothing but sin and they were covered by the lamb, so too we are covered by the blood of Jesus to atone for our sins." (Dressing Up Death.,p.86, ESV)

We are all wounded people. We don't run at all. Instead we limp along in this marathon called life. Towards the end of the marathon I ran to honor my best buddy who died. I limped along the last 6 miles. It was without a doubt the hardest thing I have ever done physically. I said Phillians 4:13 over and over. Probably thousands of times.. It became my mantra. Until the marathon I had only run 6 miles. What got me through? Love. pure and simple.

"We are all broken creatures. Everybody struggles. Beware of the believer who says, " Praise God, my son is staying out late drinking and driving. Also beware of believers who say they have never had a hardship or struggle. They are what I call super-fake believers. Maybe they have just got some bad doctrine. You know the kind I am talking about. In goes a quarter and out comes their desired product. My God is into broken things in our lives and refining us through the difficult times. God is not a sugar daddy. He is God Almighty and is interested in the here and now and future. It is called the santification process,. It is in these dark times that He grows us. We may hate this process, but when it is stripped away, He has done an incredible work in us and through us.

What do you do during these difficult days? Somedays I do nothing. Other days I spring into action, especially when it involves my child.. It is in the fire that we are growing.Check out these verses below.

"Behold, I have refined you, but not as silver I tried you in the furnace of affliction.." (Isaiah 48:10, ESV)

"Now may the God of peace sanctify you completely."
(1 Thess.5:23a ESV)

"We need to be on watch to see we are not being led astray by Satan. He is a real viable deity that is like a thief only comes to steal, kill and destroy. John 10:10, ESV). If we think he runs around in a little red outfit with horns on both sides of his head, we are very wrong. He is much smarter than that. "For even Satan disguises himself as "an angel of light." 2Corinthians 11:14, ESV).

While I am not advocating that everything bad in your life is of Satan. It is not nor would I be suggesting that it is. Just beware of him. He is the cause of many downfall of believers. For example, Billy Graham, perhaps the greatest preacher of all time, and now his son, Franklin Graham, were and are very leary of the attention of many, many women admirers because they know one little indiscretion can topple the best of ministries. Take for example. Jim and Tammy Faye Baker. Or biblically Samson and Delilah. Ministers must be on their guard. Satan loves to dismantle pastors and their ministry. One little indiscretion is all it takes. A doghouse that cost 6,000 dollars is suddenly made known when instead the money could go towards many charities, not to mention to the poor here in the United States.

We have an adversary. His name is Satan, or the evil one or the devil. He was a rejected angel cast from heaven. Could you see what heaven was like? Talk about the all- you-could-eat- buffet. The closest I could get is shrimp fajitas and a large coke to wash it down.

What part do we play in the salvation experience? We sin. Plain and simple. Yup, we sin. When we do accept Christ and His spotless sacrifice, it is God who saves us, not us.

How benevolent is God. After Adam and Eve sinned and were hiding from God, He was so good to them,He made something for them to wear. Was He mad at them. No. Was He disappointed? Maybe. God turned this setback into a comeback. Satan would not and never will win against God.He could have abandoned them for their sin. But He loves us too much to let us wander around in the muck and mire of sin and shame.

"For He has clothed me in garments of salvation.. (Is. 61:10b. ESV)

This is big. Who clothes us with garments of salvation? We don't do it ourselves. God alone does it. Who saves us? We may spend year and years looking for God. We were lost, not Him. He alone is our salvation.It is interesting that the word *garment* is used here.Remember the garments used by Adam and Eve were simple fig leaves.Then, after the sacrifice, used was a lamb, and a lamb's wool clothing is a lot more comfortable than a fig leaf. Is that a good God or what?

God could have left them in the Garden in shame, but He did not do that. He took the time to sacrifice a lamb; An unblemished lamb was sacrificed and used to "cover" or used to atone for their sins. All of heaven was looking to the cross for its' redemption .It started in the Garden and finished at the cross.

What is our place in the salvation process? We do nothing but sin.Salvation is of God, not us. Redemption is about Christ. Not us. But here's the kicker.God leaves it all to us. He is not a pushy God. he does not railroad us into something we don't want. He is a gentleman.He only goes into a relationship we want.Only when we are ready does He then come into us. He is also a patient God. He will wait for us until the day we die." Dressing Up Death, Tate Publishing, 2006,.p.86-92). That is a faithful and loving Savior. Don't you agree with me?

The Lord only disciples those who are His children.He cannot let them live lives unto themselves. If He did not love us and want to grow us, He would let us go Satan's playground. Sometimes some people think God is a vending machine. In goes the money or request, and out comes our desired response. After all, we put money in. But God is so much more powerful than their Coke menality machine. Sometimes abuses happen. Accidents, occur and diseases are terminal.

I know a gal who never had a bad thing happen in her life. She brags that the key to her good fortune is right living is the key to God's heart. Heaven help her if there is an accident or terminal illness that comes her way or by her family or friends way. She is robbing God of His omnificence. Where should we put our hope in? Christ, of course. Look at the following verses. They are super duper positive.

Think about your favorite verse. Think why you love this verse so much. Nine times out of ten,it is an encouraging verse.One way to overcome obstacles in our lives is to memorize scripture. When I ran the marathon, I said Philippans 4:13 over and over the whole 26.2 miles. It became my mantra. I ran he entire race, no walking at all. The longest I had trained for was 6 miles. So I was a little nervous. What got me through? Love did. Pure and simple. I was running for my departed prayer partner. It was the same marathon she had run while pregnant and with a small melon in her chest. She did not know she had the cancer. I had to beat her time. I did. But I did it with far less obstacles than she had. That is putting it mildly them.

Here are a couple of verses I have committed to memory. See if you like

"Though He slay me,, I will hope in Him."
"May He grant you your hearts desire and
fulfill your plans." Ps. 20:4. (ESV)"

"For I know the plans I have for you, declares the Lord, and not for evil. I to give you a future, to give you a future of hope:" (Jer. 29:11, ESV)

God became a real human being when He did not have to. He experienced real things yet He never sinned. He left the all-you-could- eat- buffet for us. He became sin for us;unblemished lamb. He is waiting for us. So we limp along in this earth trodden earth. We simply have to bloom where we are planted. For me that is a nursing home and rehab place. God is not dead. He maybe slow but never late. He can take any situation and turn it into good. We should expect no less from Jehova Rapha in our lives. No matter where we are planted. He can do anything. Work with Him and expect great things...even in the mundane.

Chapter 7

Go Tell It On The Mountain

This reminds me of the widely popular television show,"The Walton's." This popular show was about country life in the hills of Kentucky. They were poor but far from rich. They invested in people not things.Whether it was breakfast, lunch or dinner, they ate every meal together and were not lacking in topics of conversation. Whether it was Grandmother with her strokes or Mom trying to make ends meet by moonlighting as a waitress, this show was not only entertaining but educational as well. My family gathered for this drama each week as well as the Carol Burnett show. Both shows hit the spot and then my sister and I were off to slumber land. I definitely remember John Boy. Us writers got to stick together!

This chapter focuses on educating churches.The church should be the primary facilitator in educating others about depression. While this may seem unusual, why then did Christ continue to heal those that suffer from depression? It has been often overlooked by the church and may even go against its doctrine.Why shouldn't the church provide, at the very least, a list of good therapists? With 20% of women who get depression each year, why not enlist a bevy of capable counselors.

I am not saying that they advertise and put out their shingle as Christian therapists. The worst counselors I have had in recent years have been terrible Christian therapists. One was having an affair with a Christian professor. They said they were not but both divorced their spouses and married each other. Something was going on there. Not sure what. Seems too convenient to me. Another one took my book Shameless and wrote her own book on shame. Then another one was just plain terrible. The therapist I have now is super. She has been with me over two decades. She doesn't judge me but listens to me. I trust her completely. She is super duper in my book. I have grown leaps and bounds with her. She, along with my physiatrist, are on my team. I would not trade them for anything in the world. My doctor listens to me and prescribes the necessary drugs for me. They have not tried to do each other's job but work together for my sake. That along with family and close friends keep me in check. I have a great support team. They keep me going. I admonish you to go to a PhD and MD if you are feeling sad or not right. It will change your life forever. I did mine.

Why not employ a list of capable therapists and pay for the church member to go? There could be a surplus of funds just for this. It is called discretionary funds. Why doesn't the church pay for its members to go to a list of wonderful doctors and have it paid for out of that fund. But here's the kicker...they must be licensed. I knew a gal who had her master's and failed the LPC test four times. She then went to work under the umbrella of someone who had passed the LPC test. Then she moved onto the church. Never having to pass the LPC test. I would caution you to only go to LPCs, and Psychologist who are board certified to give out advice. Just because they hang their shingle out of as a Christian counselor does not qualify them as such. It is a very very slippery slope to say the least. My two doctors are Christians, but neither one crams Scripture down my throat. Beware of doctors who do; who do most of the talking; and who say right and wrong most of the time. But you do need a psychologist. PhD and medical doctor. MD. These two can work together to get you back on track.

While it is not popular to get into therapy with a physcologist and medical doctor, it is paramount to get into seeing both professionals as soon as possible. If there is any abuse in your past, it is in your best interest to go to someone you trust and can talk to. Shop around if you must. Ask your doctor. You don't have to go to the first therapist you see. Make sure it is a good fit. Make sure you do most of the talking, not visa-versa. Is he/she kind? Is he/she affordable? Tell them what you are looking for in a therapist. You will go down dark corridors with this person, so make sure this is a person who will skillfully go down with you.

> Look at the following verse and see which one is your favorite and why.
>
> Isaiah 2:2-3 " It shall come to pass in the latter days that the mountain of the House of the Lord shall be established as the highest of the mountains, and shall be lifted up above the hills."(ESV)

The Waltons were getting ready in their worship attire and attitude for the Christmas Sunday church service. Missing is only the Father. Even Granddaddy attended. But not the Father of the clan. He was ok with them attending without him. He said when they were John Boy's age they could decide to go or not to go to church. Until then they were at the mercy of the Mother of the clan. She said, "that's right. And for the next two hours we were all hers."

Read the following verses and choose one to memorize. They are about the mountains. There is something healing about being outside in the hills or mountains. Something soothing. Did not Christ retire to the mountains to be before He headed to the cross? Yes he did, maybe to talk to the Father or gather Himself before He would be murdered on the cross. I know before I had a big tennis match I would go to bed the night before and would visualize winning over and over. I visualized the balls, me bouncing them three times if i won the point and five times if I lost the point. I visualized the entire match. Getting the balls after the match I had just won and shaking the girl's hands. I played the match long before I knew who I would be playing. Yes, it was all outside.

There is something soothing about being outside. Christ loved the outdoors too. There is strength in nature. Jesus knew this.

> Isaiah 2:3a "Come, let us go up to the mountain of the Lord..." ESV)

There is something healing about being outside and on top of a mountain. Take Colorado for example. When I was married, hmm, we use to go to Pagosa Springs and to Wolf Creek Pass and ski there. My husband took me to the expert level run and off he went. I cried all the way down the black, very skilled course on my bottom. I was scared spitless. I did not talk to him for 3 days. I am much more the hiking type, with lots of breaks. And food. And drink. Well, you get the picture.

There is something majestic about mountains. Especially when you have climbed them. They become more majestic then. I never will forget my best vacation ever. It was girl scout camp. Camp Highpoint. I went with Terri when I was 9 and 10. We were at Wilemena Mountain at Camp High Point, Mena, Arkansas.

There was something about being in the forest and on the mountain that was so healing and soothing. We woke up to the mountain and said goodnight to the mountain. The wind whistled in the forest, or pine trees. We worked hard and played hard. Kept our cabins spotless, ate all our food, and were exhausted at bedtime. I can't put my finger on it, but I think it was being outdoors that healed this weary pre-teen. We sang songs by the fire and cooked our breakfast by the fire. Yep, we were warm blooded girl scouts. That was the best of times for me. That was the mountain top adventure. Then life got in the way. We grew up and those days were no more.

I started to play tennis. Big sister won state her freshman year in doubles and life would never be the same. I won all the tournaments I played when I was 10 years old as a novice player. I even won state that year. I went on to win state many times as well as high school and suddenly I was the new girl to beat in Arkansas.

I ended up 2ⁿᵈ in the Southern Tournament and won the doubles and was selected my junior year in high school to represent the South against the other sections of the US. One girl went to USC the other to CalBerkly and Georgia that we represented the South, and then there was me. If I hadn't had such success early on then I wouldn't have been so gun-ho with the tennis. I got a full ride to SMU in Dallas. Texas. We made it to the final four my freshman year. Even the CalBerkley coach told me that "she should have recruited me. " That made my whole tennis career when she said that. Never had I felt so validated in my tennis life. Yep, all the tennis was worth that one comment. That was a drop, or rather flood, for a weary traveller in this game called life.

Many many, mountaintop feelings and events. None though can compete with the salvation experience except maybe childbirth. My salvation experience I called the bathroom revival. It was cold outside maybe November and I had held it all night....so I really had to go. I prayed this simple prayer or plea. "Come inside me." That was it. No sinner's prayer or theological statement. No singing angels, so fireworks, nope not anything but the cold floor of the bathroom. I immediately stopped cheating in school and my tennis even improved. I was in it for the long haul. I was in it, the Christian walk, for life. I pledged my life to Christ. I was about seventeen years old. A definite mountaintop experience for me.

"There was an old hymn that the Waltons said on their show one Christmas morning on top of Walton's mountain..."go tell it on the mountain that Jesus Christ is born." I wish I could remember just one verse but my memory fails me. That is what we are to do... tell everyone the incredible story of Jesus' birth, life, and resurrection. That is all we are here to do. Tell others about Him. At least that has been the case for me. I have watched and watched people to see if they are genuine or not. Do they walk it or just pay cheap lip service to it? One case in point is my former youth director. I studied her for 6 years as to whether or not her faith went the distance. She now has her counseling practice and a Ph.D. in Biblical counseling. I kid her that I was the reason she went into counseling. I was a mess back in the day. She goes the distance. She is one of my favorite people. I was a sophomore and she was in her last year as our youth director and I was just a babe in the fold of God' s lamb clan.

Look at all these verses which proclaim the mountains. Which one is your favorite? What runs through all of them, or what is the common thread:

Matthew 4:8-9 "Again, the devil took him to a very high *mountain* and showed him all the kingdoms of the world and their glory. And he said to him,' all these I will give you, if you will fall down and worship me." Then Jesus said to him, " Be gone, Satan! For it is written, You shall worship the Lord your God and him only shall you serve." (ESV)

Notice a couple of things. First of all God never temps us. It is all Satan. God does allow it but it is not of God. Think back to the Garden of Eden. The serpent, the devil, or Satan, tempted Eve and she ate the forbidden fruit. Did God temp her? Absolutely not. Temptation is of Satan, not the Lord.

Luke 6:12 "...He went out to the *mountain* to pray, and all night He continued in prayer to God." (ESV)

There is something about the mountains that are healing. You, I do, feel closer to God. As I have stated earlier, camp Highpoint was my favorite place, a haven for me when I was 10 and 11 years old. I think it had to do with being outside. Then tennis took over at age 12. It too was all outside year round without indoor courts. Whether it was 100 degrees or 33 degrees, I played my entire tennis career without indoor courts until I went to college. All outdoors from age nine to twenty three. It, tennis, was a safe refuge for me. It kept me out of trouble during those teenage years. It was my love of the outdoors that God knew was my refuge. Somehow, I survived the teenage years in a small town with no indoor courts. From girl scout camp to tennis, I made it through with two refuges. Now comes the relationships that helped me navigate life's turbulent waves. People can be refuges as well.

A safe haven can also be a person. Yes, a person. I have been fortunate to have worked with two professionals the last twenty years and have been lucky to go to those dark places that produced healing. But before we go out and spill the beans to a psychologist and new psychiatrist we first have to have the right people in place. Ask around. And not merely with you, but with others. Ask the church. Every church should have a bevy of therapists it refers to. And if it doesn't work out, keep trying, same with psychiatrists. If it feels wrong then move on. You are paying for it so let your guard down and get in there to those appointments. My two doctors have changed my life for the better.

When I think of safe haven I think of a lighthouse, with red and white stripes resting just beyond the jagged rocks and having a strobe light going round and round. Vessels of all kinds, who get in trouble or distress, look for the light and lighthouse to bring them to safety. Safe haven, as I said earlier, can be a boatload of safe people that God uses in our lives for very different reasons and journeys. I wish I could tell you all about them one by one but I cannot. The love of Christ they have shown me is beyond measure. I tried in the intro to do a little in the dedication, but I fail the sincere goodness they have given me over the years. I love each of them dearly, and want them to know I have found a safe haven in them. This is truly the body of Christ. I am at a complete loss to say thank you to each and everyone of them. I have learned what is a safe haven from being in a relationship with them. I covet them and the time spent with them.

Onward ho we go. Something like that. A refuge as we have seen can be a place such as a lighthouse, a person, and a God. I will confess I go more frequently to a person rather than seek God's guidance. What about things? I think things could be a refuge. Such as drinking, drugs, and yes, even sex. Those are all addictions you might say. Well, yes, those are pure blooded addictions but they also serve in the role of addiction. God loves us too much to let us stay stuck in the cycle of abuse, such as the above addictions. It is passed down from generation to generation. It is a viscious cycle to overcome. That again, it where counseling or therapy comes in. You don't have to suffer alone. There is a church and group therapy or person just waiting for you. Get into therapy today. Find a church. Make friends today. It will take time but the payoff is huge!!!!!!!!!

Chapter 8

Walking the Path of Peace

This concluding chapter looks at peace of the elusiveness of that as it relates to depression. Whether or not the church supports this book or not, it is a fact; some of those in their congregation are depressed. This claim also takes into the fact that depression has or is visiting the staff also. Where are they to go in any given year, and especially with the virus and covid in full force, 25% of women are clinically depressed in any church today.

It has been around since the dawn of time. We like to sweep in under the carpet. Here are some verses on peace. Without it in life we turn to drugs, alcohol, people pleasing, school, work, and the list goes on and on. Read these verses on peace. Which one is your favorite? Why? Hold the phone, it is a long list but well worth it to say the least. All you have to do is read, not look up. Bear in mind your favorite two or three verses. Memorize them and put them in your bathroom, or car or on the fridge. Wherever you frequent the most. That would be the fridge for me. How about you? Hmm.

"...I will give **peace** in the land..." (Lev. 26:6, ESV)

"...countenance upon you and give you **peace**..." (Numbers 6:26, ESV)

"...for he will speak **peace** to his people..." (Ps. 85:8, ESV)

"...You keep him in perfect **peace** whose mind..." (Is. 26:3, ESV)

"...the effect of righteousness will be **peace**." (Is. 32:17, ESV)

"...is no **peace** for the wicked says my God." (Is. 57:21, ESV)

"...I will extend to her **peace** like a river.".(Is. 66:12, ESV)

"...**Peace**! Be still! And the wind cased..." (Mark 4:39, ESV)

"...go in **peace**, and be still and be healed of your disease." (Mark 5:34 ESV)

"...go in **peace**, and be healed of your disease."(Mark 5:4b ESV)

"...as it depends on you, live peaceably with everyone...(Romans 12:18 ESV)

"....My people will abide in a **peaceful** habitation." (Isiah 32:18, ESV)

"...that we may live a **peaceful** and quiet life." (1Timothy 2:2, ESV)

Peace is a real and tangible component of life. It is as real as the nose on your face. Just as real as love, forgiveness, and hope and list goes on and on... One of my favorite names of Christ is The Prince of Peace. World leaders shake hands on nuclear deals, the climate change, and world peace. Ronald Regan and Jimmy Carter were the best at negotiating peace, world peace during the late 70's and early 80's. I vividly saw my dad turn off the lamp in our den when Jimmy Carter said energy usage begins with each of us... it was the state of the union speech in late January 1977. I will never forget his love for what this U.S. president said. Jimmy Carter was royalty in our house. I have no doubt that he will meet Jimmy Carter in heaven even as I write this.

The last time I saw Martha, my best friend who was pregnant and had cancer and had chemo/radiation while with child, she was so peaceful, almost serene. We talked about what heaven would be like and how I was to be welcoming to her husband's new wife.

That is right. We actually prayed for the future new wife/mother to come. I almost gagged on that prayer.

During the time she was terminal I saw Martha do this "dance" with Christ. I call it a dance, and wrote a book about it. It was stunning. Never had I seen it before like I had with her. Here is a little bit of what I saw…

> "Sometimes we make our own heaven or hell. It is not until we stop Vacillating between fear and rejection that we can then truly move Forward to live and love and embrace all God has in store for us. We May do it with fear, but we need to do it nonetheless. If we fail to Change who we want to become, we fail to embrace of what we were Created for." *(Debbie Vanderslice, Dressing Up Death, preface.2016, Tate Publishing)*

I leave you with some writing I did after my best buddy died. You know, it has been over 20 years and I still cry like a river when someone mentions her name to me. But I am slowly learning that is ok. We all mourn on different time schedules. I told God if I ever wrote a book or books that I would mention her in each and every book I get published. And have kept that promise. Here are some writings for you to ponder. They came out of my depression. It, writing, is my safe haven for me. Always has been. What pratail is your's??? May we all find refuge in God Almighty during our dark days. These came in the midst of my deep, dark, and enlightening depression. Out of depression can come something good. Just ask me!!!!! I often refer to myself as the depression queen!!!!!!!!!

Somewhere

Somewhere along the path I lost my way. Someway along
the way I lost my hope. Somehow without my hope I found
resentment. Somehow my resentment turned to anger.
Somehow my anger grew into bitterness. Somehow my
biggeness flew into rage. Somehow my rage consumed me.
Somewhere in the rage, I blamed you, O Lord, For all the pain.
For all the abandonment.

For all the fear.
For all the sorrow.
For all the fears. For all the tears
For all the dreams never filled,

For all the hopes left unfulfilled.

Do you know O God, how difficult this is for me?

To take your hand and trust you in what I cannot see?

You know my past and pain so well,
For it is real to me.
Can you take my tattered life
And help me to live for all eternity?
Somewhere O Lord,
I gave my heart

Somewhere along the trodden road O Lord,
I lost those that I loved.
If I give you my honesty

And choose to do what is right

Will you in turn give me the strength

To last the good and holy fight?
Because I come before you as a little child
So very, very lost,
Somewhere along the way, I blamed You

For all the pain and thus the cost.

(Debbie Vanderslice Dressing Up Death, (Debbie Vanderslice Tate Publishing ESV 2006, p. 40)

Well, I am afraid that this is the end of the road for us. Christ is our safe refuge. No matter who we are, or what we have done, He alone makes us worthy. He is our refuge, just like our mentors or family is...we can always go to Him. We can either blame Him and turn to a life of sin or we can dig our heels in and trudge on ahead, one foot in front of the other. HE ALONE IS OUR REFUGE.

Printed in the United States
by Baker & Taylor Publisher Services